Dedication

This book is dedicated to my ancestors and my Orisha.
Thank you.

...and to my mother who is also my best friend, my sister
and our midnight conversations, to my grandmother. I
love you. Micheal and Wanda my inspiration.
To my support system Leslie, Therese, Adam, Valeary and
of course my dear friend Micheal.

When I Look in the Mirror...

A Guide for developing positive
Self Image and knowledge.

Written by
Sopoeia Greywolf

Illustrated by
Chris Hall

with an introduction
by Oswald Gift

Published by
A&B BOOKS PUBLISHERS
Brooklyn, New York, 11201

Text copyright ©1993 by Sopoeia Greywolf.
Illustrations by Chris Acemandese Hall.
Illustrations copyright ©1993 by *A&B BOOKS PUBLISHERS*.
Introduction for parents and young readers copyright © 1993 by Oswald Gift.

Printed in the United States of America

Published by:

A&B BOOKS PUBLISHERS
149 Lawrence Street
Brooklyn, New York
11201 (718-596-3389)

First Printing 1993

ISBN: 1-881316-28-9

10 9 8 7 6 5 4 3 2 1

Introduction

When I Look in the Mirror is an outstanding introduction for developing *positive self image and positive self knowledge* (esteem) for our young heroes[1]. This book is a guide for helping parents and young readers alike to see and develop the beautiful creative aspects that lie deep within themselves.

When I look in the mirror uses positive self images of *Blak[2] Melanin people* to bring out the differences in skin shades, facial tones and all the inert attributes that make us so different and so special. We are truly the first *designed of god*. Therefore, we are truly indeed a very special people.

This book calls to attention parent and young reader alike to look deep within themselves and to espouse the creature nature of the *Most High* in us all. My young Prince and Princess, take *A look in the mirror* and you will see somebody. You will see you, the first manifestation of the *Most High* to create the human race.

Just look *in the Mirror* and say "I am beautiful and I am a very special person." To the parent we can turn back the cycle. Please **try** and let the young ones know that they are beautiful and beauty lie deep within each of us, beauty lies deep in the soul, beauty reigns in the light brown, dark brown and in the helios of our soul.

I say *when I look in the mirror* my sister, my brother, my spouse, my son and my daughter *I see the real me*. I see a strong positive *Melanin man*. I see the *divine creation* of the first man; A *Blakman*, a sun man, a sol[3] man, a sol 'o' man: *the wise man, is truly* the *blakman*.

Oswald J. Gift.
Oct 16, 1993.

---

1 Hero   Initial word incorporated both sexes: her, he

2 Black   Original spelling. Middle English < Blak , means:to gleam, radiant, white orig.: sense Webster New World Edition Simon & Schuster.

3 Sol   Spanish lit., sun: from radiant sun.   Webster New World Edition Simon & Schuster

When I look in the mirror

What do I see ?

Brown skin
as Brown as can be
Set in honey caramel ice cream
That's what I see

When I look in the mirror

What do I see?

Hair so curly it's like a spring
Round and round, up and down
How fun it is to have hair like spring

I See a gift from God for my mommy and daddy

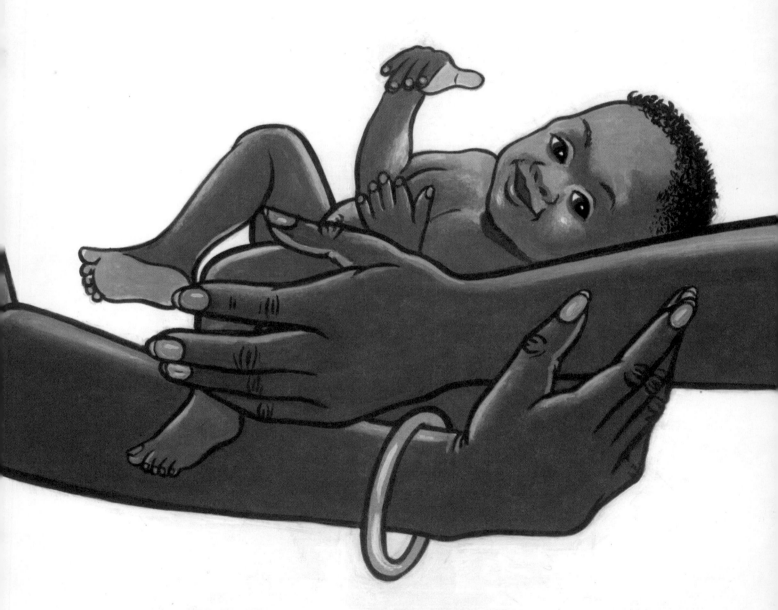

That's what I see!

Cheeks so round and chocolatey
with just a touch of cherry jubilee

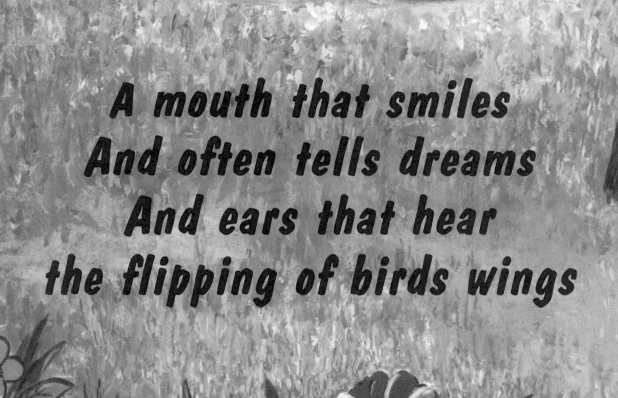

A mouth that smiles
And often tells dreams
And ears that hear
the flipping of birds wings

Feet and hands
and many other things
And I shout out
"This is who I'll be
This is me"

A nurse, a doctor,
a piece of poetry

When I Look in the mirror

What do I see?

I see my grandma,
my grandpa and my Aunt Bea
I see all of the people that have
ever loved me,
Inside of me

Eyes which set
in the sun
like brass rings
Yes that's what I see

I see somebody
I see me

How I like looking in the mirror at me

About The Author

Sopoeia Greywolf was born on December 10, 1970. She grew up in Brooklyn, New York and has been writing since age nine. The main focus of her writings is to teach children to believe in themselves: for if any one can believe in themselves, they can certainly reach their *goals*. As a testimony to this, Sopoeia who has suffered from dyslexia has continued to *set and reach her goals*. Besides writing, she is a self-made business woman and has opened t he first Native American shop in Brooklyn: *"Seven Drums"*. Sopoeia has graduated from the Brooklyn College Conservatory of Music, and intends to further her studies in classical music at the Manhattan School of Music.

About The Artist

Artist Chris Ace-mandese Hall born in Florida. A graduate of Stanton High School-Jacksonville, Fla. A graduate of the School of Visual Arts-N.Y.C. Chris is one of the original members of AJASS (African Jazz-Arts Society & Studios Inc.). Chris is a music lover and Jazz fan. His lyrics to Miles Davis' tunes "So What", "Bitches Brew" and Coltrane's "Tranes Blues" were recorded b y the father of vocalese - Eddie Jefferson.

Some of his renditions of paintings, creations & designs includes: The Magic Crown Video, Little Zeng's ABC (World's first Blactk *Super-Griot-Hero*), Original Huggy Bean Doll (Golden Ribbon Playthings), Let's Celebrate Kwanzaa and countless paintings & illustration for other books and Art shows.

A&B BOOKS PUBLISHERS is committed to the education and economic development of our community. Our titles reflect this commitment, we are overwhelmingly anxious to bring forth adults and children titles.

Children's Titles

AFRO-TOTS ABC	3.95
AFRO-TOTS 123	3.95
AFRO-TOTS Shapes and Color	3.95
AFRO-TOTS Metamatics	3.95
Once upon a Kwanzaa	5.95
What Color Is God?	5.95
Little Zeng ABC	4.95
When I Look In The Mirror	5.95

Comic Book Titles

Electro-X   1,2 & 3
Sectornauts 1,2 & 3
Femme Fatale 1 & 2

Please Look forward for our upcoming series

SMART START

Send For Our Complete Catalog
A&B BOOKS PUBLISHERS
149 Lawrence Street, Brooklyn,
New York 11201
(718) 596-3389